Steck

WORLD MYTHS

Wanjiru Brings the Rain

Reviewer
Abdullahi A. Ibrahim
Fellow, Institute for the Advanced Study and Research
of the African Humanities, Northwestern University

STECK-VAUGHN
COMPANY
A Subsidiary of National Education Corporation

ISBN 0-8114-3370-6
Copyright © 1994 Steck-Vaughn Company.
All rights reserved. No part of the material protected by this copyright may be reproduced or utilized in any form or by any means, electronic or mechanical, including photocopying, recording, or by any information storage and retrieval system, without permission in writing from the copyright owner. Requests for permission to make copies of any part of the work should be mailed to: Copyright Permissions, Steck-Vaughn Company, P. O. Box 26015, Austin, TX 78755. Printed in the United States of America.

1 2 3 4 5 6 7 8 9 0 SEC 99 98 97 96 95 94 93

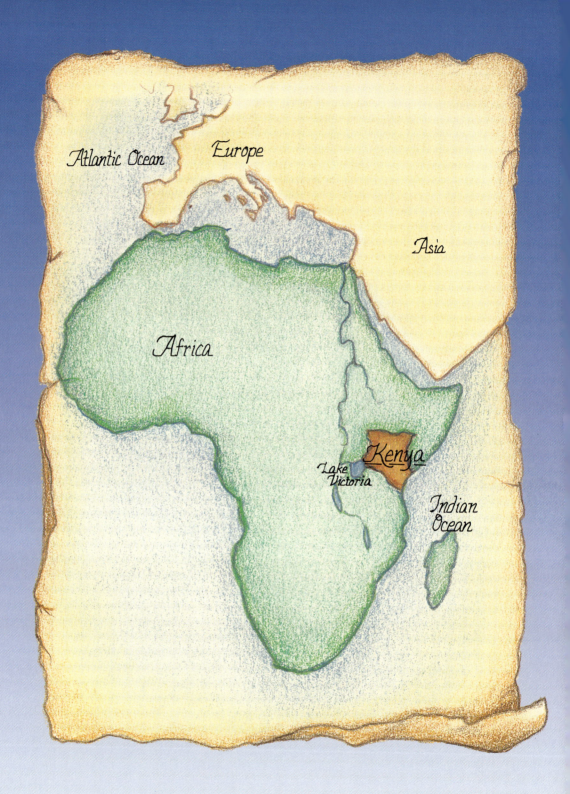

Introduction

The country of Kenya in East Africa runs from Lake Victoria east to the Indian Ocean, as you can see on the map on page 2. There are more than thirty different groups of people living in Kenya, including the Kikuyu (kik OO yoo), Masai (mo SIE), and Kamba (KOM buh). Each group has its own language and culture. The largest of these groups is the Kikuyu who live in the south central highlands near Mount Kenya. The myth you are about to read comes from the Kikuyu.

The Kikuyu people have traditionally lived by growing crops. In fact, one of their myths tells of how the creator god invited the ancestors of the Kikuyu, the Masai, and the Kamba each to choose one of three things—a bow, a spear, or a digging stick. The Kamba's ancestor picked the bow, and those people became hunters. The first Masai took the spear and went to the plains to herd cattle. But the ancestor of the Kikuyu chose the digging stick and learned how to practice agriculture.

In this story, you'll meet a character who takes a great risk for the sake of love. What else can you learn from the myth about the way the Kikuyu people think humans should treat one another? How might the story of Wanjiru (won JEE roo) have been different if the creators of the myth had known about irrigation?

Wanjiru Brings the Rain

For three years, no rain had come to the land around Mount Kenya, the Mountain of Whiteness. The blazing sun beat upon the earth. The mountain forests of figs, evergreens, and bamboos turned brown. Streams and rivers dried up. Even the mighty river that flowed from the highlands to the sea in the east was nothing but a trail of dust. Elephants, rhinos, and buffalo wandered the grasslands looking for water.

As always, the people had planted their crops of millet, beans, and sweet potatoes around the slopes of the mountain. But for three years, they had watched as the plants wilted and died in the terrible drought. Without rain, the people suffered greatly from thirst and hunger.

The people looked at the mountain and prayed to the great god, who had created the world and made the mountain his resting place.

   But their prayers did not
make the rain come. They knew that
something else had to be done. From all around, the
clans came together in a large open space on a hilltop to
discuss the problem. "Why does the rain not come?" they asked
each other. "Have we angered our ancestors in some way?"

But no one knew the answer. So they called for the rain maker and asked him the same question.

After a long time, he answered. "There is a young woman among us," he said. "She is called Wanjiru (won JIR oo). Her family must be honored with gifts if rain is to fall. Two days from now, return to this spot. Each of you, young and old, must bring a goat for the family of Wanjiru."

Two days later, all the people returned to the clearing, each herding a goat. Wanjiru's kin stood in a circle in the center of the clearing with Wanjiru in the middle.

Wanjiru looked around nervously. "How am I to bring rain?" she thought. "I am not a god. Yet I must believe that somehow I can help my people."

She waited while thousands of people gathered around her and her relatives. There were so many that they all could not stand in the clearing. Some waited on the slopes of the hill.

Their chatter and the bleating of their goats broke the stillness of the heat. Everyone was excited and hopeful that rain would finally come to the land that had been dry for so long.

The first person came forward to present a goat to Wanjiru's father. But before her father could even reach out to accept the gift, something strange happened.

Wanjiru cried out in terror, "Help me! I am sinking!"

Everyone turned to see that Wanjiru's feet had sunk into the hard, dry earth. While they watched, she continued to sink up to her knees!

Her mother and father saw this. "Wanjiru is sinking! We must help her!" they cried as they rushed forward.

But the people pushed in around them and offered them the gifts of the goats, which were very valuable. "Do not touch her!" the people yelled. "She is sinking into the earth, just as the rain will come and soak into the earth."

Wanjiru was now in the earth up to her waist. She stretched out her arms to the people gathered around her.

"Save me!" she cried out to them. "Rain will come soon. It will come! You must save me!"

Wanjiru sank in up to her chest, but the rain did not come. "Please! Help me! You will see! The rain will come! Help me!" she begged.

Her family heard these woeful pleas. But each time they moved to help her, the crowd gave them more goats. So they stopped trying to rescue her.

Now Wanjiru sank to her neck so that only her head remained above the ground. She began to weep. And as she wept, she heard the faint sound of rolling thunder far away. Wanjiru looked at the sky and saw dark, gray storm clouds slowly moving in from the horizon. "You see! The rain is coming! Now you can help me!" she called to the people.

But the people paid no attention to her. They all stood, staring with hopeful faces at the darkening sky. A curtain of cool, moist air swept over the hilltop and lifted the blanket of dry heat.

The first drop fell on Wanjiru's forehead. But her face was already damp with tears.

A moment later, the storm broke. Rain fell in great drops, and the parched ground soaked it up. The people began to sing and dance in celebration, while Wanjiru sobbed in despair. "Will my own people let me sink into the earth?" she cried.

Some members of Wanjiru's family moved forward again to save her. But as before, the people pressed them back and gave them goats. The people were afraid that if they rescued Wanjiru, the rain would stop.

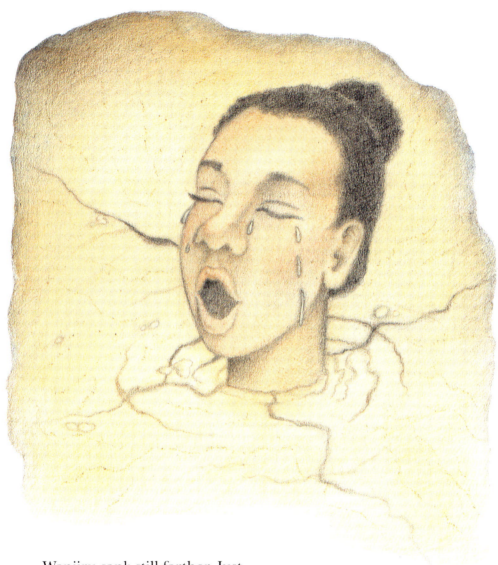

Wanjiru sank still farther. Just before she was swallowed up by the earth, she cried out for the last time. "I am lost! My own people have done this!" she wailed. Then she disappeared, and the earth closed over her.

The rain fell steadily and heavily. Lightning flashed and thunder echoed. The people ran from the hilltop to take shelter in their homes. Wanjiru's family also returned to their homes, leading their goats.

When everyone had left, one young man remained on the hilltop. He loved Wanjiru and had tried to push through the crowd to help her. But he could not reach the inner circle.

Now he stood and looked at the spot where Wanjiru had vanished into the earth. "Wanjiru is gone and her own people have allowed it to happen," he cried in his grief. "But I will not abandon her. I will enter the earth and find her."

He went home and got his shield and spear. Then he returned to the hilltop and stood upon the spot where Wanjiru had stood. Just as she had sunk, he also began to sink until he, too, was swallowed up by the earth.

When the ground closed over his head, he found himself on a long road. He walked along in the silent darkness until he finally came upon Wanjiru.

She was in a miserable condition. Her face wore long lines of sorrow. She was hungry and weak, and her clothing was torn and bedraggled.

The warrior wept in love and pity for her. "Wanjiru, you were left to die because the people wanted rain," he said. "Now the rain has come. I will take you back with me."

Then he gently lifted Wanjiru and carried her like a child on his back. They traveled over the long road below the ground. Together they rose up until they stood once more on top of the ground.

"I cannot return you to your family or your people," the warrior told Wanjiru. "They have treated you shamefully. But I will take you to the home of my mother and take care of you."

Wanjiru agreed. She was angry with her people and grateful to her friend, the kind warrior.

When night fell, the warrior carried Wanjiru to his mother's home. He set Wanjiru down outside the house and entered. "Please leave for awhile, mother," he said. "I have business to do here that no one may see."

His mother refused to leave her house. "What are you hiding from me, son?" she asked. "I am your mother. You can trust me."

So the warrior told her how he had rescued Wanjiru. He made his mother promise not to tell anyone that Wanjiru had returned from below the ground.

Then the young man brought Wanjiru inside the house, and he and his mother cared for the poor young woman. Wanjiru ate and soon regained her strength. She dressed in lovely clean clothes made of goatskin.

Then one day the people held a great dance to celebrate the return of the rain. It took place at the hilltop clearing where Wanjiru had sunk into the earth.

Wanjiru did not want to go to the dance where she would see the people who had refused to save her. But the young man and his mother persuaded her to go, after all.

The young man went ahead. He moved through the crowd, looking and listening. He found that the people had forgotten all about Wanjiru. He said nothing to anyone about her return.

When everyone had gathered at the clearing, and no one remained at home or appeared on the roads, Wanjiru and the young man's mother came out of the house. They walked to the clearing and joined him at the celebration.

13

Wanjiru was soon recognized by her relatives, who were surprised and thrilled to see her. "It is Wanjiru! We thought that we had lost her! How wonderful that she has come back among us!" they all cried as they ran forward to greet her.

But the young man pushed them away and reprimanded them. "You would not help her when she needed you!" he yelled at them. "You let her sink into the earth because you wanted some goats. Even when the rain came down, you did not pull her from the ground! You do not deserve to have her back. I love her, and so I rescued her. I will take care of her. Now, go away and leave her alone as you did before!"

Then he and Wanjiru and his mother went back to their house. For several days, he refused to let Wanjiru's family see her. But they kept coming and begging to speak with her and ask her forgiveness.

Finally, he and Wanjiru gave in. "Wanjiru and I forgive you because you are her family," he said. "You may see her."

Soon after that, the young man and Wanjiru were married on the hilltop where Wanjiru sank into the earth and brought rain back to the people.

Glossary

agriculture *n*. Farming; the raising of crops for food and other uses.   p. 3

bedraggled *adj*. Wet and dirty as if dragged through mud. p. 10

irrigation *n*. System of ditches to supply water to fields for growing crops.   p. 3

kin *n*. Relatives; family.   p. 6

millet *n*. A kind of grain.   p. 4

parched *adj*. Very dry and thirsty.   p. 8

reprimand *v*. To scold or blame.   p. 14

rhino *n*. A rhinoceros, which is a large animal with one or two horns on its snout.   p. 4

shamefully *adv*. In a way that brings shame; wrongly. p. 12

woeful *adj*. Sad; heartbreaking.   p. 8

Acknowledgments

Steck-Vaughn Company

Executive Editor   Diane Sharpe
Senior Editor   Martin S. Saiewitz
Assistant Art Director   Cynthia Ellis

Proof Positive/Farrowlyne Associates, Inc.

Program Development, Design, Illustration, and Production